Judith Weiss-Katz

A HAND IS FOR

Illustrated by
Sofia Iudina

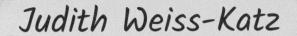

Archway Publishing books may be ordered through booksellers or by contacting:

Archway Publishing
1663 Liberty Drive
Bloomington, IN 47403
www.archwaypublishing.com
844-669-3957

Because of the dynamic nature of the Internet, any web addresses or links contained in this book may have changed since publication and may no longer be valid. The views expressed in this work are solely those of the author and do not necessarily reflect the views of the publisher, and the publisher hereby disclaims any responsibility for them.

Any people depicted in stock imagery provided by Getty Images are models, and such images are being used for illustrative purposes only.
Certain stock imagery © Getty Images.

Interior Image Credit: Sofia Iudina

ISBN: 978-1-6657-2475-3 (sc)
ISBN: 978-1-6657-2584-2 (hc)
ISBN: 978-1-6657-2476-0 (e)

Print information available on the last page.

Archway Publishing rev. date: 06/21/2022

Dedicated to my dear husband
Eugene Katz

A hand is for saying how do you do?

A hand can hold something bright and blue

With your hands you can draw, or tickle your toe

The policeman's hand tells the traffic to slow
and when to stop and when to go

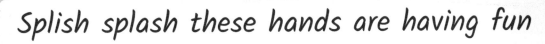

Splish splash these hands are having fun

Some hands throw a baseball and some swing a bat

Some hands can scratch puppies or pet a black cat

Hands can sit quietly in your lap

Pockets are places for hands to hide

Hands button your jacket or get your shoes tied

Hands come in colors - in many different styles

Hands come in sizes - dads, moms, and childs

You can keep your hands busy from morning till night
as long as you teach them to do what is right

Finger-paint or make mud pies, build castles of sand

Just remember you never should hit with your hands!

Judith Weiss-Katz is a children's advocate and a former member of CASA (Court Appointed Special Advocate). She and her husband are the active grandparents of 21, and also have 21 great grandchildren. Judith taught pre-kindergarten for several years; she started college in her 40s and graduated with a Bachelor of Arts in psychology.

Printed in the United States
by Baker & Taylor Publisher Services